T0126065

Volando bajito

VOLANDO BAJITO

Volando bajito

Little Low Flying

poems

Alicia Partnoy

Translated by Gail Wronsky
Illustrated by Raquel Partnoy

Red Hen Press 🐓 Los Angeles

Volando bajito

Cover art: "Tina Modotti" by Raquel Partnoy

Book design by Michael Vukadinovich
Cover Design by Mark E. Cull

ISBN: 1-59709-002-6

Library of Congress Catalog Card Number: 2005901777

Published by Red Hen Press

The City of Los Angeles Cultural Affairs Department, California Arts Council, Los Angeles County Arts Commission and National Endowment for the Arts partially support Red Hen Press.

First edition

Acknowledgments

Mi inmensa gratitud a mi madre Raquel Partnoy, por prestarme sus obras para ilustrar esta edición y a Gail Wronsky por construir el puente del lenguaje.

Agradezco a las siguientes revistas culturales y literarias, donde muchos de estos poemas fueron publicados por primera vez, tanto en su versión original como en traducción: *Feminaria, Puentes de la memoria, La Triple Jornada, The Los Angeles Review, Mind and Human Interaction, Pool, International Poetry Review*.

Mi agradecimiento también a las siguientes antologías:*A Chorus for Peace: A Global Anthology by Women,* Marylin Arnold, y otros. comp.(University of Iowa Press: Iowa City, 2002) y *Mujeres mirando al Sur: Antología de poetas sudamericanas en USA,* Zulema Moret, comp. (Ediciones Torremozas: Madrid, 2004).

El poema *"Calles"* de Evangelina Arce se publica con la autorización de su autora, a quien agradezco profundamente..

La versión en inglés de "Little Dissertation On The Subject/Object" de Gail Wronsky fué publicada en *Dying for Beauty* (Copper Canyon Press: Washington, 2000).

El original en inglés de "10" de Ruth Irupé Sanabria fué publicado en *Poets Against the War.* Sam Hamill, Sally Anderson y otros, comp. (Thunder's Mouth Press: New York, 2003).

"The Voice of the Innocent" de Bernice Johnson Reagon y Alicia Partnoy ha sido grabada como canción en el CD *The Women Gather. 30th Anniversary.* Sweet Honey In The Rock. (EarthBest, 2003).

"Arte poética" fué publicado en mi poemario *Venganza de la manzana-Revenge of the Apple* (Cleis Press: San Francisco, 1992).

My immense gratitude to my mother, Raquel Partnoy, for lending me her artwork to illustrate this book, and to Gail Wronsky, for building the language bridge.

Thanks to the following journals and cultural magazines, where many of these poems were first published either in Spanish or in English: *Feminaria, Puentes de la memoria, La Triple Jornada, The Los Angeles Review, Mind and Human Interaction, Pool, International Poetry Review*.

I also want to thank the following anthologies: *A Chorus for Peace: A Global Anthology by Women.* Marylin Arnold and others, ed. (University of Iowa Press: Iowa City, 2002), and *Mujeres mirando al Sur: Antología de poetas sudamericanas en USA.* Zulema Moret, ed. (Ediciones Torremozas: Madrid, 2004).

The publication of the poem *"Streets"* has been authorized by the author, my deepest gratitude to Evangelina Arce.

"Little Dissertation On The Subject/Object" by Gail Wronsky was published in *Dying for Beauty* (Copper Canyon Press: Washington, 2000).

"10" by Ruth Irupe Sanabria was published in *Poets Against the War.* Sam Hamill, Sally Anderson, and others, ed. (Thunder's Mouth Press: New York, 2003).

"The Voice of the Innocent" by Bernice Johnson Reagon and Alicia Partnoy was released as a song in the CD *The Women Gather. 30th Anniversary.* Sweet Honey In The Rock. (EarthBest, 2003)

Arte poética" was published in another translation in *Venganza de la manzana-Revenge of the Apple* (Cleis Press: San Francisco, 1992).

Contents

III

Diálogos para levantar vuelo
Dialogues for Raising Flight

Contents

III

Diálogos para levantar vuelo
Dialogues for Raising Flight

A la memoria de Blanca Ciammaichella y Ernesto Malisia, porque se les fue la vida trabajando por la recuperación de la voz de los vencidos.

To the memory of Blanca Ciammaichella and Ernesto Malisia, because they spent their lives working to recover the voice of the defeated.

Translator's Note

When *The Little School*, Alicia Partnoy's book of stories and testimonial prose about her abduction and incarceration as a *desaparecido* in an Argentinean concentration camp, was published in 1986, it was read by people in the English-speaking world who were experiencing peaceful times, relatively speaking, in terms of history. Terrorism was a thing not much talked about, not feared by people in New York who had yet to learn its horrors, or in London where the bombings of World War II were fairly comfortably far behind. Likewise when her book of poems, *Venganza de la manzana/Revenge of the Apple*, was published in 1992, its concerns: torture, exile, military oppression, seemed remote enough to English-language readers that the poems could be accommodated. These good poems, powerful poems, important poems, could be read here in the States as testimony from a faraway place, descriptions of experiences, thank god, we'd never really have to know much more about.

But so much has changed.

The world into which *Volando bajito/*Little Low Flying arrives is a world in which the torture perpetrated by U.S. soldiers against Iraqi prisoners is unavoidably documented. It is a world in which we are aware that American citizens can be seized, interrogated, and imprisoned for political activity, religious affiliation, or ethnicity. It is a world in which we palpably fear annihilation on our worst days, and thoughtfully consider the violence of our species and the gaping distance between our own values and those of our government on our better days. It is a world which needs the insights, the power, the authority, the wisdom, and the beauty of Alicia Partnoy's writing more than ever.

Partnoy has lived in the U.S. for over two decades, making her truly an American writer, South *and* North. While South American and Latin American writers have had historically as subject matter the failures of the nation-state, the battle of the individual against political coercion, and the military occupation of their home territories, North American writers, at least those writers most representative of the dominant culture, have not. The United States has not "lost" its wars. Its Constitution guarantees the rights of its citizens against would-be tyrants and oppressors. Young women living ten miles outside of El Paso, Texas, are safe from abduction, disappearance, murder—are they not?

Much has changed. There is a new generation of readers who understand how desperate is the need to confront and understand issues that people in other parts of our world have long confronted and understood. So it is not only with pleasure as a poet and a reader of poetry but with urgency as a citizen and activist that I introduce this book.

Little Low Flying had originally as a subtitle "The Poetics of Defeat." The title itself, which suggests both flying under the radar and keeping a low profile in English, refers most literally to the political context out of which the poems are written. In Argentina, Partnoy was a member of a political group which opposed a military dictatorship now recognized world-wide as an illegitimate and oppressive regime. Through the assassinations, disappearances, and torture of 30,000 people—political activists as well as many people who were not remotely involved in politics—the dictatorship defeated its opposition.

What does it mean to be defeated? How does an artist summon the strength, the desire, the belief in oneself which is necessary for the creation of art? How do you speak when you've been prevented from speaking? How do you see when you've been blindfolded? How do you fly? You fly, Partnoy tells us, a little low.

One of the shortcomings of the English language is that we don't have anything comparable to the Spanish diminutive "ito." Our diminutives, such as "ette" as in kitchenette, are straightforward. They lack the subtlety and ambiguity of the Spanish form. "Ito" in Spanish is at the same time an intimacy, an endearment, and neither. *Volando bajito* means flying a little bit low, flying humbly, close to the ground, not soaring, and it doesn't. Because the poems in this book do soar. The poems in this book are not humble, except insofar as humility is a part of their charm. They put guns to the heads of assassins, as in "Balancing." They are "a walking scream," as in "Spanish Lessons." They cry "No!/at the invasion of jackboots and shrapnel" ("Experiment").

The poetics of defeat, as this book tells us, is a poetics of strength, of necessary outrage, and of hope that the defeat will not go unrecorded, unrecognized by the machinations of human history. The poetry of defeat is more urgent than the poetry of success. Wallace Stevens says this: "Death is the mother of beauty," reiterating John Keats' assertion that autumn, the time of the year which represents dying, is the most fruitful time. Here, in "The Art of Poetry," Partnoy puts it her way—succinctly and gorgeously:

> That which flies low
> is my poetry.
> Dredging the odors
> deep within grassland.
> I don't look for height.
> Vertigo of soaring.
> I assault the distances

flying low.
There is the word,
the little forgotten one,
fresh and with roots
or redolent of fear.
Iridescent thing
like the meat
of a cadaver, turning
into seed.

The terse sensuality of these poems—their gentleness and unflinching courage in the face of devastation, of genocide—, is so much more than instructive. It is edifying. It is inspiring. It is poetry in its deepest and truest sense. Poetry with the moral imperative of spiritual law. Poetry with the subtlety and insight of our greatest resources, intelligence and compassion. Readers in the United States, a culture which despises and fears defeat as much as it celebrates and adores domination, have much to learn from these poems—among other things, that *low* flying is a skill to be cultivated, and that the true artistic voice cannot be silenced by guns and tanks and jackboots. Defeated things, if they are tended to, can shimmer, can grow "a pair of crazy feathers"("Ars . . ."),can scream.

My fear in translating these poems was that some of Partnoy's strength, some of her, at times, most forceful and beautiful music, some of the sly humor, the self-deprecating refusal to say too much, to speak for others, would be watered down, would be somehow delayed or de-positioned. I feared that in speaking for her through the translations I would distort her voice. I feared both overstating and understating. English, it seems to me, is a less subtle language than Spanish. It is, in the very least, less charming and musical. It has the ham-fistedness of the Germanic languages. The constraints of what is recognizable and acceptable to readers of the contemporary American lyric poem also seemed imposing. Would the poems seem too fragmentary? Too direct? Too quick in their juxtaposition of, for example, maternal tenderness and an unabashed hostility toward oppressors?

Finally, however, two things saved me. First, the fact that I had Alicia Partnoy herself, who is quite fluent in English, as a consultant on the translations, and second, I suppose, my own subversive tendencies as a poet—my own belief that what is recognized from one moment to the next as poetry in this country is something we, as poets, should constantly challenge and question. And so, I have tried to allow the poems to speak for themselves as much as possible. To be as bold as they are, to be as unafraid as they are to utter what might be uncomfortable, or unapologetically difficult, truths.

Mothers are left with gravestones which in no way resemble their dead children ("Voice of the Mother"); political exiles will never really comprehend where they are, even if they find one another ("Reunion"); the ability of human beings to torture other human beings is so intrinsically human that it is built into our language ("Torture Machine: Vocabulary"); in some places in the world, women carry onions in their pockets to reduce the effects of tear gas ("Old Jerusalem: Chronicle of the Intifada"). These things are true. It is necessary for us to know them. And only a poet of Alicia Partnoy's great skill, great ear, great eye, and enormous heart could have rescued them from the lowlands of defeat and given them to us in such compelling and immediate form.

—Gail Wronsky

I

Poéticas de la derrota
The Poetics of Defeat

Experimento

Tómese con cuidado una palabra,
la palabra 'miedo', por ejemplo.
Rocíesela con los sabores
salobres y amargos de la huída.
Estrújesela con dedosgarfios
contra la boca misma del estómago.
Un revoltijo imposible en las entrañas,
la certeza de que le falta el piso,
una marea blanca en las pupilas
y el aire cortajeado a cuchillazos.
... Y si el experimento no le
                        resultara,
        abra grande la boca y grite: ¡No!
        a la invasión de botas y metrallas.

Experiment

Take, carefully, a word,
the word 'fear,' for example.
Sprinkle it with the brackish
and bitter flavors of escape.
Squeeze it with iron fingers
into the mouth of the stomach.
Revulsion in the viscera,
no sure floor on which to stand,
a white tidal wave in the pupils,
the air ripped up by giant daggers.
. . . If the experiment doesn't yield
                            results,
                open the mouth wide and cough out: No!
                at the invasion of jack-boots and shrapnel.

Arte poética

Eso que vuela bajito
es mi poesía.
Rastreadora de olores
dentro del pasto.
Yo no busco la altura.
Vértigo el vuelo.
Embisto la distancia
volando bajo.
Allí está la palabra,
olvidadita,
fresca con las raíces
u oliendo a miedo.
Tornasoleándose algo
como la carne
cadáver que transita
a la semilla.

The Art of Poetry

That which flies low
is my poetry.
Dredging the odors
deep withing the grassland.
I don't look for height.
Vertigo of soaring.
I assault the distances
flying low.
There is the word,
the sweet and forgotten one,
fresh and with roots
or redolent of fear.
Iridescent thing
like the meat
of a cadaver, turning
into seed.

Ars ...

A toda derrota
alguna vez le crecen
un par de locas plumas
una flor confundida
en el costado
abierto una
        perla despistada
en el pescuezo
cerca del grito
vos
tu voz
    tu voz
      tu voz
¡Ay
sementera de sal
      c
        u
          á
            n
              t
                o
                    nos duele!

Ars ...

Every defeat
at some point grows
a pair of crazy feathers
a cursed flower
on the flank
slit open
        a disoriented pearl
at the throat
next to the screaming
voice
your voice
    your voice
       your voice
Ay
fields sown with salt
       h

         o

           w

             m

              u

                ch

                   hurts us!

...POÉTICA

Escribo rescatando sedimentos:
una piedra una lata oxidada
un caracol quebrado una sandalia viuda
un cofre de tesoro pirateado
y a veces
un cadáver.
Lo traigo a superficie, lo reanimo,
lo despierto
a golpe de verbo y adjetivo
y entonces
—casi siempre—
él me juega la mala pasada de esfumarse
al más leve contacto con mi verso.

. . . Poetica

I write by recovering sediments:
one stone one rusted can
one broken shell a widowed sandal
a coffer of pirated treasures
and sometimes
a corpse,
which I bring to the surface, reanimate.
I wake it
with a slap of verb and adjective
and then
almost always
it does me the dirty trick of disappearing
at the slightest contact with my poetry.

II

DERROTEROS DE VIDA
TRACKS OF LIFE

ROMANCE DEL PRISIONERO

Que por mayo era, por mayo,
cuando hace la calor,
cuando los trigos encañan
y están los campos en flor,
cuando canta la calandria
y responde el ruiseñor,
cuando los enamorados
van a servir al amor;
sino yo, triste, cuitado,
que vivo en esta prisión;
que ni sé cuándo es de día
ni cuándo las noches son,
sino por una avecilla
que me cantaba al albor.
Matómela un ballestero;
déle Dios mal galardón.

       Anónimo
       S XIV

ROMANCE DE LA PRISIONERA

Que por enero, era enero,
cuando hace la calor,
cuando el viento se arrecuesta
en el salitral en flor,
cuando cantan los gorriones
responde nuestro dolor,
cuando los enamorados
dan su sangre por amor;
sino yo, sobreviviendo
en esta triste prisión;
sostengo que es de día
cuando a claras noches son,
sino por una avecilla
que gritó revolución.
Matáronla los milicos;
déles Dios mal galardón.

       Alicia Partnoy
       S XXI

ROMANCE OF THE PRISONER

It was May, yes, May
when the heat is in the air
when the wheat forms its stalks
and the fields are full of flowers,
whe the lark sings
and the nightingale answers,
when the lovers
go and bow down to love;
but I, sad wretch
live behind bars
know neither the day
nor the nights' stars,
except by a bird
that sang to me at morn.
A crossbowman killed it;
God give him his reward.

>   Anonymous
>   14th Century

ROMANCE OF THE PRISONER

It was January, yes, January,
when the heat is in the air
when wind blows hard
through the blossoming salt marshes,
when sparrows sing
and our sorrow answers,
when lovers
spill their blood for love;
but I, surviving
in this sad prison,
I swear it is daytime
when clearly it is still the night,
all because of a small bird
that shouted revolution.
Soldiers killed it;
God give them their reward.

>   Alicia Partnoy
>   21st Century

PRESA POLÍTICA

Cómo explicarle señora celadora
si usted me pesca así en este momento,
"consolándome" de la falta
de noticias de afuera
con un cilindro gordo de papeles
protegidos con nylon
                    y mi dedo . . .
Cómo explicarle señora celadora
                    que no,
que yo a mi hombre me lo sueño,
al mundo, si cuadra, me lo invento,
y al análisis de coyuntura
lo alojo -con placer, a qué negarlo-
en los dos agujeros más leales
del escondite que es mi propio cuerpo.

POLITICAL PRISONER

How to explain it mistress prison guard
if you catch me right now in the act,
"consoling myself" for the lack
of news from the outside
with a fat cylinder of papers
protected by plastic wrap
                    and my finger . . .
How to explain it mistress prisonguard
                    that no,
I am only dreaming of my man;
as for the world, if I want, I invent it,
and having taken stock of the situation,
I accommodate it—with pleasure, why
should I deny it—
in the two most faithful holes
of the hiding place which is my own body.

Habitación a la calle
(Postal de Washington)

Busqué en tu cuerpo
un país
(el nuestro, el mío).
Busqué . . .

mientras la 16 corría
medio loca de autos
hacia la Casa Blanca.

A tientas sobre el exilio
busqué en tu voz
acentos,
los sonidos de casa.

Las riendas perdí
(los dos perdimos)
por cabalgar a tientas
sobre el exilio.

La 16 corría
jineteada de autos
hacia la Casa Blanca.

Living at Street-level
(Postcard from Washington D.C.)

I sought all over your body
a country
(our country, mine).
I sought . . .

While 16th Street ran
half crazy with cars
all heading for the White House.

Feeling my way above exile
I sought in your voice
accents,
sounds of home.

The reins lost
(we both lost them)
for riding our way
over exile.

16th Street ran
ridden jockey-like by cars
all heading for the White House.

Pregunta semiculinaria

Cómo me desexilio sin romperme
como tomate gordo en la ensalada
sin desangrarme contra las lechugas
en semillas pequeñas y doradas.
Cómo me desexilio
y huelo a rico
y a fresco y a crocante
y a pan nuevo.
Cómo me desexilio y no me comen.
Cómo me desexilio y sigo entera.

QUESTION SEMICULINARY

How do I de-exile myself without breaking
like a fat tomato in the salad
without bleeding all over the lettuce
in small golden seeds.
How do I de-exile myself
and smell tasty
and stay fresh and crunchy
like new bread.
How do I de-exile myself without being eaten.
How do I de-exile myself and come out whole.

Voz de la madre

Después de todo aquello
volver a la palabra
como si no doliera
decir, amor: la muerte
nos hizo zancadillas
contra los eucaliptus
y hay un mármol que nombra
los ojos de tu hijo
como si le cupieran
mi amor, adentro suyo.

Voice of the Mother

After all that
to turn to the word
as if it doesn't hurt
to say, love: Death
cornered us
against the eucalyptus trees
and there is a stone that names
the eyes of your son
as if they fit,
my love, inside it.

Clases de español

I.
Escribo en la pizarra:
calabaza
mate
tango
gaucho
des-
aparecido
cosmopolita
ciudad de Buenos Aires
30.000
Islas Malvinas
Gabriela Sabatini
campos secretos
de detención
Evita
Maradona
dictadura militar
tortura

El programa lo indica claramente:
Laboratorio de idiomas—
Video 1:
Un paseo por latinoamérica
Primer segmento.
Tema: Argentina.

SPANISH LESSONS

I.
I write on the blackboard:
gourd
mate
tango
gaucho
dis-
appeared
cosmopolitan
city of Buenos Aires
30,000
Falkland Islands
Gabriela Sabatini
secret detention
camps
Evita
Maradona
military dictatorship
torture

The syllabus clearly indicates:
Language lab—
Video 1:
A Stroll Through Latin America
First section.
Subject: Argentina

II.
Este semestre
el programa exige
enseñar al estudiante el verbo "ser"
en los distintos tiempos
del modo subjuntivo:

Si fuéramos o fuésemos
una generación
que no hubiera o hubiese
sido destrozada,
si yo no fuera
un grito caminando,
si no estuvieran
(verbo también prescripto este semestre)
mis venas anudadas
por el dolor de la pérdida
de amigos, hermanos, compañeros . . .
si fuera mi demanda:
"que la justicia sea"
al menos escuchada . . .

no hubiera sido,
alumnos, necesario
inquietarlos con este par de clases
impregnadas del tufo de la muerte.

II.
This semester
the syllabus requires
teaching the students the verb "to be"
in the various forms
of the subjunctive mode:

If we were or had been
a generation
which weren't or hadn't
been destroyed
if I were not
a walking scream
if it weren't ("to be" in the
continuous present:
verb also required this semester)
my veins knotted
with pain, with the loss
of my friends, brothers, *compañeros* . . .
if my demand:
"that justice be"
had been heard . . .

it wouldn't have been
necessary, my students,
to disturb you with these couple of classes
impregnated with the stench of death.

REENCUENTRO

Te espero en la barrera en la que el sueño
arrincona al pasado.
Tenés domesticadas
todas las alas locas de tu sangre.
Me hablás de tu inocencia
como de un niño muerto.
A la ciudad le crecen las colinas:
presiente algún milagro.

A la hora de irnos, despertarnos,
el viejo pulóver destejido
del recuerdo se me enreda en las manos.

La ciudad nos conmina a despedirnos.

A la hora de irnos,
despertarnos,
sin milagros,
no sabemos muy bien por qué llegamos.

REUNION

I wait for you at the gate where dreams
give way to our past.
You have domesticated
all of the crazy wings of your blood.
You talk to me about your innocence
as if it were a dead child.
In the city which is building hills:
anticipation of a miracle.

At the hour of our going, our waking,
the old unraveled pullover
of memory tangles in my hands.

The city summons us to separate.

At the hour of our going,
our waking,
without miracles,
we don't really know why we've arrived.

Respuesta

¿ . . . y vos
COMO TE SALVASTE?

Es casi
acusación.
Es lápida.

Se me congelan
las ganas de contarte
lo de aquellos
que no fueron salvados,
lo de
ZulmaMaríaelenaBenjayBraco
MaryNestorGracielaRauleugenio
y el
proyectodeliberacionacional.

Yo
no me salvé.
Me salvaron

Response

. . . and you?
HOW DID YOU SAVE YOURSELF?

It's almost
an accusation.
It's a slap of concrete.

It hardens my desire
to tell you the stories
of those
who were not saved
of
ZulmaMariaelenaBenjayBraco
MaryNestorGracielaRauleugenio
and the
programofnationaliberation

I
didn't save myself.
What saved me

los pies caminadores
de mis padres,
los pies que daban vuelta
a la Pirámide,
las manos
que escribieron una carta,
la "sol
i dar
i dad"
de la Cecilia
y el cachetazo a tiempo
de la suerte,
el dedo de algún dios
desprevenido,
la decisión
de un tribunal de asesinos
que como
dice siempre
don Emilio
estará registrada en microfichas

y escondida en alguna caja
fuerte
que se resiste
a todas las Pandoras.

Y ¿por qué me salvé?
Ahora andá y preguntales
a ellos, los milicos.

Ellos sí saben.

were the feet of my parents
walking,
the feet that circled
the Pyramid,
the hands
that wrote a letter,
the "sol-
i-dar-
i-dad"
of Cecilia
and the time-strike
of luck,
the finger of some
oblivious god,
the decision
of a tribunal of assassins
which
don Emilio
always says
was registered on microfilm

and hidden in some box
so strong
it could keep out
all the Pandoras.

So, why was I saved?
Why don't you go there
and ask them, the *milicos*.

They know.

PINTANDO MURALES

Por tus manos me apropio las paredes
del Barrio, ésas que voy perdiendo.
Mi garganta te grita ese amarillo.
Soles tus veinte años lo traducen
en círculos y arcos
rayos, cortinas y hasta algún
sombrero.
Pasan ellos, los invasores,
como las "Instamatics"
les cliquean los ojos.
Yo quiero que les pegue tu amarillo
pero el color, a veces, sólo canta bajito.

Painting Murals

Through your hands I take over the walls
of the barrio, those being taken away.
My throat shouts your yellow.
Suns your twenty years have transformed
into circles and arcs,
rays, curtains, even a certain
hat.
They go past, the invaders,
like "Instamatic" cameras
they click their eyes.
I want your yellow to strike them
but the color, I'm afraid, sings just a little too lowly.

Torture Machine: Vocabulario

severe and prolonged. . . :
amputation of. . . :
picana eléctrica:
¿qué se siente
cuando
el idioma de uno
es el único
adecuado
para nombrar
wet submarine. . . :
potro:
no vergüenza
no culpa
burns:
la bandera. . . :
¿qué
se siente?
parrots perch:
sexual torture:
teléphono:
rápido
a corregir
no hay
ph
en
español
pero . . .
apollo: . . .
diagnosis of . . . :
falanga:
portugués
ellos
¿qué
sienten?

Torture Machine: Vocabulary

severe and prolonged ... :
amputation of ... :
picana:
what does one feel
when
one's language
is uniquely
appropriate
for naming
wet submarine ... :
potro:
no shame
no blame
burns:
the flag ... :
what
does one feel?
parrots perch:
sexual torture:
teléphono:
quick
to correct
there's no
ph
in
Spanish
but. . .
apollo ... :
diagnosis of ... :
falanga:
Portuguese
them
what
do they feel?

black slave:
cachots noirs:
o
¿qué . . . ?
el quirófano:
sí dolor
los franceses

sí miedo.
Dice el Mingo que es como si miles de terminaciones de cables eléctricos
te tironearan de la carne.

Una mujer
con los labios pintados
de azul
le explica
al público
"el dolor físico no solamente
se resiste a ser verbalizado
sino que
destruye el lenguaje,
inmediatamente lo
revierte
al estado previo al lenguaje
a los sonidos y gritos
que profiere el ser humano
antes de aprender
la lengua"
le petit déjeuner . . . :
le déjeuner: . . .

black slave:
cachot noirs:
or
the French
what . . . ?
the operating room:
yes pain

yes fear
El Mingo says it's as if thousands of electrical cable endings
jerked your flesh out.

A woman
lips painted
blue
explains it
to the public
"physical pain does not simply
resist language
but
actively destroys it,
bringing about an inmediate
reversion
to a state anterior to language,
to the sounds and cries
a human being makes
before language
is learned"
le petit dejeuner: . . .
le dejeuner: . . .

le rodeo: . . .
cajones: . . .
¿qué?
. . .
. . .
. . .
plantón:
. . .
pie
¡dad!

le rodeo: . . .
cajones: . . .
what?
. . .
. . .
. . .
guard:
. . .
have pity!

La Vieja Jerusalén:
Una crónica de la Intifada (1987)
A Rachel Corrie en el 2003

Lastiman de tan blancas
las piedras ancestrales.
Se quiebran
bajo el peso
de tres manchas de sangre.
Fue aquí donde Jesús
supo de las espinas.
Sobre esa misma piedra
los soldados arrastran
el cuerpo castigado
de un palestino más.
¿Qué hacen estas mujeres?
¿Qué quieren ver?
¿Por qué
desde tan lejos vienen
trayendo lápices libretas cámaras ojos?
¿No han descubierto aún las extranjeras
la inmensa utilidad de las cebollas?
Les lastima la sangre
sobre las piedras blancas
y el cuerpo castigado de un palestino más.
De pronto gritan: ¡Basta!
Toda la gente se une
y en un sincronizado movimiento
visten los uniformes
máscaras antigases.

OLD JERUSALEM:
CHRONICLE OF THE INTIFADA (1987)
To Rachel Corrie in 2003

So white they hurt,
these ancestral rocks.
Crushed
under the pressure
of three drops of blood.
It was here where Jesus
knew thorns.
Over the same rock,
soldiers drag
the punished body
of one more Palestinian.
What are those women doing?
What do they want to see?
Why
do they come from so far away
bringing pencils notebooks cameras eyes?
Havent' these foreigners discovered
the enormous usefulness of the onion?
The blood on white rocks
and the punished body of one more
Palestinian hurts them.
Suddenly people shout: Enough!
Everyone unites and
in one synchronized movement
men in uniforms
put on their gas masks.

Entonces todo rueda
corre
se avalancha
lloran los ojos
lágrimas químicas
y del caos rociado
de hortalizas heridas
panes catapultados
fuera del territorio del pequeño mercado
y entre todos los cuerpos
que el miedo anda empujando
surge, salvadora,
la mano de una anciana
que me pone en la mano
un trozo de cebolla.
Aprendo entonces, aprendemos todas,
que aquí en Jerusalén,
a diferencia de cualquier lugar del mundo
la cebolla es remedio
que detiene las lágrimas.

Then everything turns
runs
avalanches
the eyes cry
chemical tears
and out of the sprayed chaos
of bruised produce
catapulted loaves of bread
far beyond the territory of the little marketplace
out of the crowd of bodies
which fear pushes here and there
a savior emerges,
the hand of an old woman
who puts in my hand
a piece of onion.
Then I learn, we all learn,
that here in Jerusalem,
as opposed to any other place in the world
onions are antidotes
for detaining tears.

ALIENACIÓN

A Daniel
A Tede

Hay quienes cometen la crueldad
de morirse antes de que tengamos
el tiempo necesario para responderles
la carta que escribieron o el pedido
de comentar el poema que dejaran
en su última visita a nuesta casa.
Se trata casi siempre de hombres ávidos
de atención, cariño, recono
      cimiento,
y eso se nota en la manera clara
en que nos informan de su muerte incipiente
y en su foma grácil de abandonar el barco
dejándonos solos, pasajeros de la culpa.

ESTRANGEMENT

For Daniel
For Tede

There are those who commit the cruelty
of dying before we have
the time needed to respond to
the letter they've written or the request
for a comment on the poem they left
on their last visit to our house.
It's almost always a case of men eager
for attention, affection, re-
        cognition,
and we can see this in the obvious manner
in which they inform us of their ensuing death
and in the fine way they abandon ship
leaving us alone, passengers of guilt.

BALANCE

al Mingo (padre de Eva Victoria
y Anahí Paz)

De la victoria nos queda solamente
el nombre embanderado
de nuestra hija
escrito bajo la sombra amarga
de aquellos compañeros
que no llegaron siquiera a la derrota
con la sangre en el cuerpo.
Y de la paz, amor, sólo no queda
el nombre entre palomas
de nuestra hija
y la memoria del sueño de la bala
al centro de la frente
del asesino.
De la justicia

Balancing

*to Mingo (father of Eva
Victoria and Anahi Paz)*

Of victory what remains for us is just
the name of our daughter,
emblazoned,
written under the bitter shadow
of those *compañeros*
who didn't make it to the defeat
with blood in their bodies.
And of peace, my love, what remains for us
is just the name of our daughter
among the doves
and the memory of the dream of the bullet
in the center of the forehead
of the assassin.
Of justice

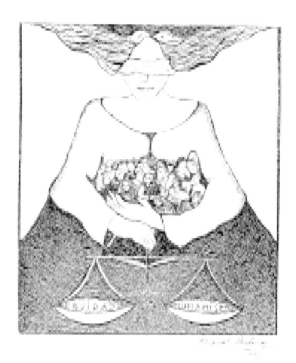

En Rocha y la vía

Cuando todo se acabe,
Antonio Leiva,
nos venimos a vivir
    a Buenos Aires
porque está lleno de la gente
    y de las cosas
que ya nunca jamás encontraremos
y todo queda a la vuelta
    de la esquina
como tu rabia y la mía
    y la derrota
viaja como cualquiera en el sesenta
y no se baja nunca.
    No se baja.

In the Middle of Nowhere

When it's all over,
Antonio Leiva,
we'll go to live
    in Buenos Aires
because it's full of the people
    and the things
we'll never ever find
and everything stays
    right around the corner
like your fury and mine
    and defeat
travels like someone on the #60
and doesn't ever get off.
    Doesn't get off.

Latina al fin del milenio
(Canción)

Si me muero con la M, montonera
y trastabillo en la S, sandinista,
¿será que me caeré del alfabeto
si renazco en la Z, zapatista?

Abrazada a la bandera que me quiera,
a las brazadas en la tierra que me asista,
abrasada en el dolor de cada cuerpo
que sufra la saña imperialista.

Este año 2000 con tantos ceros
es el fin de algún milenio y el principio
de otra lucha por no ser sólo un agujero,
hueco en la historia, un número en la lista.

END OF THE MILLENNIUM LATINA
(A song)

If I'm murdered with the M, Montonera,
if I stumble into S, Sandinista,
will I somersault out of the alphabet
if I come back in Z, Zapatista?

Embrace of the flag that's in love with me,
fruit of the land that provides for me,
inflamed by the pain of each person's body
that suffers the spit flames of imperialism.

This year 2000 with its many zeros
is the end of some millennium and the start
of another struggle against being hollow,

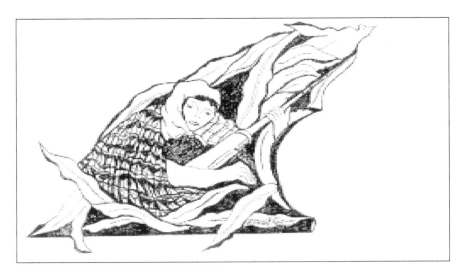

III

Diálogos para levantar vuelo
Dialogues for Raising Flight

A Carlitos alláendevoto

¿Dónde la
democracita?

¿cuándo los
derechísismos humanos
y por qué la liber
tad tan cerce
nada?
Huele a asfalto caliente
hay mucha reja
desde donde yo miro
a
buenos
aires.

To Carlitos Indevotoprison

Where's that
sweet little democracy?

when
human mega-rights
and why a lib-
erty so stripped to
nothing?
It reeks of hot asphalt
there's a lot of iron
in the way of my view
of
buenos
aires.

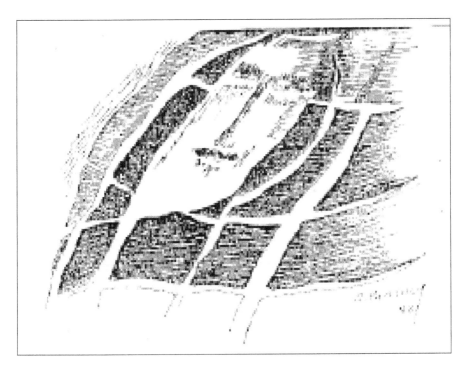

Diálogo con Alaíde Foppa

No se puede vivir
Con una muerte dentro:
hay que elegir
entre arrojarla lejos
como fruto podrido
o al contagio
dejarse morir
                    —*Alaíde Foppa*

Busco el espíritu de esta mujer
y encuentro:
su amor por las manzanas,
su ansiedad de alelíes sobre el pecho,
los cinco hijos que amasó
su cuerpo
su cuerpo desgajado en la tortura.
Alaíde de alas y de ideas
cuando arrojo lejos de mí tu muerte
se vuelve proyectil
por la justicia.

Dialogue with Alaíde Foppa

No one can live
with a death inside:
you have to choose between
tossing it far away
like a rotten fruit
or keeping it
and dying from contamination
                                    —Alaíde Foppa

I try to find the spirit of this woman
and discover:
her love of apples,
her lust for holding gilly flowers
to her heart,
five children kneaded
by her body
her body ripped apart by torture.
Alaíde of ideas and of flying
when I toss your death far away from me
it turns into
a meteor of justice.

THE VOICE OF THE INNOCENT/
LA VOZ DE LOS INOCENTES

*A Song by Bernice Johnson Reagon
and Alicia Partnoy*

Tuvimos las manos limpias.
Mientras los asesinos disfrazaban
a golpes de cal nuestras paredes
blanqueando consignas, sangre, sueños,
sobrevivieron nuestras manos limpias.

Our hands were clean.
While you painted white walls in our streets,
we kept our hands clean.
While you tried to erase our past and our blood,
our clean hands survived.
While you whitewashed our slogans
our blood our dreams. . .

We have not killed anyone.
We have not tortured anyone.
We have not taken work from the people.
I have not starved and sold the children.
We have not brought our country to ruin.

No matamos a nadie.
A nadie torturamos.
Tampoco le quitamos al pueblo su trabajo.
No he vendido, no he matado de hambre
a los niños.
Ni arruinamos la patria.
Our hands are clean.

Te conjuramos con nuestras manos limpias,
General de la muerte, Señor del hambre.

It is only we who must run our lives.
Y es que somos nosotros
los únicos capaces de regir nuestras vidas.
Let it be known to those who hear this song.

Let it be known the wearing thin of our patience.
Y si las manos limpias no bastaran
las mancharemos con flores de rabia.
No he vendido, no he matado de hambre
a los niños.
Tenemos las manos limpias.
Our hands are clean.

Palabras por Silvia

Ese señor de libretita en mano,
ese señor de credencial al cuello,
ese señor que quiere hablar conmigo
y no ve a Evangelina
no la ve
parada sobre lo seco de su duelo
con la incertidumbre de quien lo sabe todo
porque es madre de desaparecida
que ayer nomás aquí
aquí fincaba
y ese señor
quiere que yo le cuente de bahía
blanca ciudad al centro de otros vientos
esta mañana de sábado en la plaza
de armas tomar evangelina arce.

Nadie es profeta en su tierra evangelina.

Señor, ahora estoy muy ocupada
y Evangelina sabe que ella no existe
y está plantada allí sobre su grito
y ese señor no escucha a Evangelina
como tampoco escuchan muchos de ellos.
Y Silvia Arce es aquí y ahora,
es Juárez y es mordaza.

Yo sé, señor, se torna una rutina,
ya noesnoticia simprelasmismasmuertas.

WORDS WRITTEN FOR SILVIA

That gentleman with the little notebook in his hand,
that gentleman with credentials at his neck,
that gentleman wanting to talk with me
he doesn't see Evangelina
doesn't see her
standing the dry ground of her sorrow
with the uncertainty of someone who's totally clear
because she is the mother of a disappeared girl
who dwelled here
just yesterday
and that gentleman
wants me to tell him about *bahia*
blanca a city in the center of other winds
this Saturday morning in the *plaza*
de armas evangelina arce is ready to take up arms.

No one is prophetic in this land *evangelina.*

Right now I'm very busy, sir,
and Evangelina knows that she doesn't exist
and yet she's sitting there on top of her scream
and that gentleman doesn't listen to Evangelina
the way he doesn't listen to so many others.
And Silvia Arce is here and now
it's Juarez it's a wad of cloth in the mouth.

I know, sir, it becomes routine,
it's no longer news, always-the-same-dead-ones.

Pero señor de libretita en mano,
pero señor de credencial al cuello,
haga el favor y mientras yo termino
de copiar los versos que tarjó esta madre
sobre las hojas de su cuaderno ocre,
haga el favor de oir a Evangelina
pedir justicia.

Escuche aquí y ahora
antes de que los huesos de su hija
nos lo demanden.

Ciudad Juárez, México. 1 de junio de 2003

But gentleman with little notebook in hand,
gentleman with credentials at the neck,
do me a favor and while I finish
copying verses this mother tatooed
over the pages of her ochre journal,
do me the favor of hearing Evangelina's
claim of justice.

Listen now and here
before the bones of her daughter
demand it.

Ciudad Juarez, Mexico. June 1, 2003

CALLES
Poema de Evangelina Arce,
madre de Silvia Arce

Por las calles de Juárez
ya no se puede andar
porque no sabemos quién
anda atrás de nosotros
para podernos atacar.

Somos madres ofendidas
que a nuestras hijas nos
han arrebatado   que no
sabemos adónde se las
llevaron.

Son gente de alto poder
como trabajan en el gobierno
se creen personas que todo
puen hacer.

Secuestran jóvenes   violan
y matan   las tiran en el

desierto como un animal
como son federales no se
les puede castigar.

Yo sufrí un atentado
por hablar y pedir
justicia   por eso el gobierno
nos manda intimidar
pero miedo no les tenemos
justicia es lo que queremos y
se aclaren
todos los crímenes de
mujeres   por eso es que
gritamos justicia.

STREETS

Poem written by Evangelina Arce,
Silvia Arce's mother

We cannot walk the streets
of Juarez anymore
because we don't know who
is walking behind us
is waiting to attack us.

We are offended mothers
whose daughters
have been kidnapped   who don't
know where they've been
taken.

They are high and mighty people
because they work in the government
they think that
they can do anything.

They seize young girls   rape them
and kill them   throw them in the

desert like animals
and because they are *federales*
no one can punish them.

I was attacked
because I talked asked
for justice   for this the government
sends them to intimidate us
but fear we don't feel
justice is what we want
that they reveal
all the crimes against
women   this is why
we shout for justice.

Se hicieron denuncias y
desplegados por todo el
mundo y todos los estados
pidiendo protección y justicia

que el gobierno nos ha negado

yo no me puedo callar
a mi hija quiero encontrar
los federales que se la
llevaron que la vengan entregar   justicia.

30 de abril de 2003

Denouncements were made
and ads were displayed
all over the world all over the states
asking for protection and justice

that the government has denied us

I cannot shut up
my daughter I want to find
the *federales* who took
her must bring her back   justice.

April 30, 2003

Los molinos de la memoria

Frente al campo de concentración La Escuelita de Bahía Blanca, donde estuve desaparecida durante la dictadura militar allá por el setenta y siete, había un molino roto. Los milicos lo habían atado con alambre. A los conscriptos del Comando del V Cuerpo de Ejército les tocaba hacer guardia "imaginaria" allí y eso los aterrorizaba. Resulta que en las noches sin viento el molino se desataba y echaba a girar solito. Cuenta la leyenda, que es siempre la verdad, que los espíritus de los desaparecidos movían las aspas.

En 1998, veintidos años después de ser liberada, volví al sitio de La Escuelita. Ví el molino pero los espíritus de mis amigos del alma, la Vasquita y la Corta, María Eugenia y Néstor, de mis compañeros María Elenita, Graciela (la embarazada que dió a luz en cautiverio), Benja, Braco . . . sus espíritus no echaron a girar las aspas. En cambio, viajaron conmigo hasta mi casa de Los Angeles.

Días después, cuando iba en bicicleta al trabajo me *pedalié* un poema. Cuando lo ví sobre la página me dí cuenta de que tenía forma de revólver. Recordé entonces aquellos versos de Gabriel Zelaya: "la poesía es un arma/cargada de futuro" y entonces me pregunté:

The Windmills of Memory

Across the road from the secret detention center the Little School, where I was 'disappeared' in 1977, there was a broken windmill. The military had tied it up with wire. Young draftees were terrorized when forced to stand on guard there. They knew that even on calm, breezeless nights the windmill's blades would break loose and rotate on their own. Legend had it—we all know legends tell always the truth, that the windmill was moved by the spirit of the disappeared.

In 1998, twenty two years after my release from The Little School I went back to the site of the concentration camp. I saw the windmill but the spirit of my soul mates, Vasquita, Corta, María Eugenia and Néstor, and those of my other *compañeros* María Elenita, Graciela (who gave birth in captivity), Benja, Braco…their spirits did not move the windmill. Instead, they followed me to my house in Los Angeles.

A few days later, while going to work on my bike, I *rode* a poem. When I saw it on the page I realized it was shaped as a gun. I remembered the lines by the Spanish poet Gabriel Zelaya "Poetry is a weapon/loaded with future." Then I asked,

¿. . .y si el arma, Zelaya,

                  apuntara al futuro?

¿Sobre qué muertos echaremos qué culpas
cuando se nos desteja la trama del silencio?
¿Cuáles serán las puertas para la cruz de sangre
y cuáles las solapas de estrellas amarillas?
¿De qué gargantas frías rapiñaremos voces
para que sean el eco de lo que dijo el amo?
¿Qué perdón, qué "justicia humanamente posible"
atarán
con alambre
los molinos
de nuestra
memoria?

. . . the weapon, Zelaya,
what if it's aimed at the future?

Upon what dead shall we place what blame
when the warp and woof of our silence is unwoven?
What doors will be chosen for the cross of blood
and which will be the lapels for the yellow stars?
From what cold throats will we scavenge voices
in order to echo what the tyrant said?
What pardon, what "humanly possible justice"
will bind
with wire
the windmills
of our memory?

Little Dissertation on the Subject/Object (fragment)

Gail Wronsky

v. Dinner with the Argentine Poet

however, convinced her that disappearance
as a metaphor
was morally insupportable.
She would have to try to learn another
talent. She would have to
try to learn to be, again.
To be in the body, not in the slant
of its shade; to be in
the eyes and not in some huge room
behind them; conspiring.
To leave behind her death mask
of unrivaled beauty,
the transparencies that got her
through the day —what would be left?
The imperfection of her virtues,
the confusion of the undraped corpse,
eyes which deny the I-I, the doubleness of
misperception. Here's to nothing that is not
inmediately knowable as love or art,
she said, toasting the woman from Argentina.
Here's to watermelon, said the woman,
this rich, red fruit
split open on the table between us,
having lived for nothing ever but to
reproduce itself.

Breves elucubraciones sobre el sujeto/objeto (fragmento)

Gail Wronsky—Traducción de Alicia Partnoy

v. Una cena con la poeta argentina

la convenció, sin embargo, de que la desaparición
como metáfora
era moralmente insostenible.
Tendría que tratar de adquirir
algún otro talento. Tendría que
tratar de aprender a estar, de nuevo.
A estar en el cuerpo, no en el sesgo
de su sombra; a estar
en los ojos y no en una pieza enorme
detrás de ellos, conspirando.
Si dejara atrás esa su máscara de muerte
de sin rival belleza,
esas transparencias que la guían
de la mañana a la noche ¿qué quedaría?
La imperfección de sus virtudes,
la confusión del cadáver sin mortaja,
ojos que niegan la duplicidad del yo, la doblefaz del
equívoco. Brindemos por nada que no sea
conocible de inmediato como el amor o el arte,
dijo, levantando su copa hacia la mujer de Argentina.
Brindemos por la sandía, dijo la mujer,
por la riqueza de la fruta roja
partida sobre la mesa entre nosotras,
y que no ha vivido nunca para nada
más que para reproducirse.

Promesa urgente a una niña de Bagdad

Por doce ojivas vacías
revienta el cielo en tus manos,
ruge el señor de la guerra
de rostro y gestos humanos.
Sobre el filo de la tierra
tus hermanas, tus hermanos,
barricadas de clemencia,
impotentes levantamos.
Ba
rrica
das
de
clemencia
im
potentes
le aventamos.

La guerra
Anahí Paz Leiva Partnoy,
8 años-Traducción de Alicia Partnoy

La guerra es terrible.
Disparar de armas
caer de bombas
uno puede morir
o con suerte
sólo lastimarse
y no morir.
Y lástima te han de dar
los que arriesgan sus vidas
por tu seguridad.

Pues a ser inteligentes
y no ir a la guerra, gentes.

An Urgent Promise to a Girl in Baghdad

Translated with Eva Victoria Leiva Partnoy,
13 years old

Due to those 12 empty warheads
the sky bursts in your hands,
the master of battle is roaring
his face and gestures like man.
And on the edge of the earth
we, your sisters and your brothers
clemency barricades
powerless we gather.
Cle
men
cy
barricades
with
power
we throw at them.

War

Anahí Paz Leiva Partnoy,
8 years old

War is terrible.
Guns shooting,
bombs falling,
you can die
or if you are lucky
you can just get hurt
and not die.
So you should be sorry
for the ones that risk
their lives for your safety.

So be smart
and don't go to war.

10 (Fragment)

by Ruth Irupé Sanabria,
27 years old

10.
to be honest with you I don't care how pigeons live or think
I'm really thinking how *paloma* means pigeon and *paloma* means dove
how *dove* symbolizes peace but *pigeon* is a ubiquitous element of the human
landscape and how the two meanings are not synonymous
in this language

10 (FRAGMENTO)

Ruth Irupé Sanabria,
27 años—Traducción de Alicia Partnoy

10.
si he de ser honesta con vos no me importa cómo viven o piensan las palomas
pero me pongo a pensar que *pigeon* quiere decir paloma y *dove* quiere decir
paloma,
y que *dove* simboliza paz y *pigeon* es ubicuo elemento del paisaje humano
y en cómo los dos significados nos son sinónimos
en este idioma

S.O.S

Quién pudiera agarrarte por la cola
magiafantasmanieblapoesía.
Quién pudiera agarrarte por la cola,
acostarse contigo una vez sola
y después olvidar esta manía.
—Juan Gelman

. . . Si nunca tuvo cola mi poesía
decime, Juan, cómo la cazo ahora.
Si sólo fue una boca con encías
abiertas al tumulto de la ola.
Si fue un ojo redondo que velaba
por la seguridad de su cardumen,
un manojo de escamas entrenadas
en sacarle el cuerpo a los anzuelos.
Pasame Claribel de los Umbrales
esa receta eterna contra la sequía
        del verso.
Contame vos, María,
cómo le saco el trapo a la pecera.
Si nunca tuvo cola, si sólo era
reflejo de ese grito de la gente,
espejo que nadó contra corriente
        empecinado en esquivar las redes
        preciosas
        de la canción de gesta.

S.O.S.

Who could ever catch you by the tail
magicghostfogpoetry.
Who could ever catch you by the tail
make love to you just once
and then forget about this craze.
—Juan Gelman

. . . since my poetry has never had a tail,
tell me, Juan, how should I catch it now?
Since it was just a mouth, its gums
opening to the tumult of the wave.
Since it was a round eye keeping watch
for its school,
a handful of scales trained to
shepherd the body away from hooks.
Give me Claribel of Thresholds—
your ageless recipe against the drying up
        of poetry.
And you must tell me, Maria,
how to lift the night-cloth off the fishbowl.
 . . . Since it never had a tail, since it's only been
a reflection of a shout of the people,
a mirror which moved against the current
        avoiding like hell the precious
        nets
        of the heroic epic.

Notas

"ROMANCE DE LA PRISIONERA"
La versión del poema anónimo es del libro *Flor nueva de romances viejos* de Ramón Menéndez Pidal.(Espasa-Calpe: España, 1967).

"RESPUESTA"
Cecilia (Vicuña) escribe sobre las 'palabrarmas,' una de ellas es "sol-i-dar-i-dad: dar y dad sol."
Emilio (Mignone), a cuya memoria dedico este poema fue padre de una desaparecida argentina y valiente abogado que luchó por los derechos humanos. Pirámide (de Mayo): Monumento en Buenos Aires. Desde 1977 las Madres de Plaza de Mayo han marchado todos los jueves alrededor del mismo.

"TORTURE MACHINE: VOCABULARIO"
Lista extraída de *Forced Out:The Agony of the Refugee in Our Time* por Carole Kismaris y William Shawcross. (Random House, 1989).Tomado del libro de documentación del Simposio "Confronting Political and Social Evil," Tufts University, 1991. El texto entre comillas es mi traducción de una cita de Elaine Scarry en *The Body in Pain. The Making and Unmaking of the World* (Oxford University Press, 1985, pág. 4).

"LA VIEJA JERUSALEN:UNA CRONICA DE LA INTIFADA (1987)"
En 1987 viajé con una delegación de escritoras para levantar testimonio de la represión contra el pueblo palestino. Descubrimos allí, por experiencia propia, que el oler un trozo de cebolla disminuye los efectos de los gases lacrimógenos. Rachel Corrie, una joven heroína de los Estados Unidos, fue asesinada en el 2003 por una topadora cuando trataba de evitar la demolición de viviendas palestinas que llevaba a cabo el estado de Israel.

"DIALOGO CON ALAIDE FOPPA"
Alaíde Foppa, poeta, periodista, crítica de arte, feminista, madre y luchadora de la resistencia guatemalteca fué secuestrada por las autoridades de Guatemala a los sesenta y seis años, el 19 de diciembre de 1980. Murió en la tortura.

Notes

"ROMANCE OF THE PRISONER"
This version of the anonymous poem is from the book *Flor nueva de romances viejos* by Ramón Menéndez Pidal.(Espasa-Calpe: Spain, 1967).

"RESPONSE"
Cecilia (Vicuña) writes about word-weapons, one of them is "solidarity," when you divide it in syllables, it means in Spanish "to give and give sun."
Emilio (Mignone), to whom I dedicate this poem, was the father of a disappeared woman and a courageous human rights lawyer.
Pyramid: since 1977 the Mothers of the Disappeared have been marching around this monument in the Plaza de Mayo, Buenos Aires, Argentina.

"TORTURE MACHINE:VOCABULARY"
The list is from *Forced Out: The Agony of the Refugee in Our Time* by Carole Kismaris and William Shawcross (Random House, 1989), excerpted from the conference hand-out for the Symposium "Confronting Political and Social Evil," Tufts University, 1991. The text between quotation marks is from *The Body in Pain. The Making and Unmaking of the World* by Elaine Scarry (Oxford University Press, 1985, page 4).

"OLD JERUSALEM: CHRONICLE OF THE INTIFADA(1987)"
In 1987 I traveled with a delegation of women writers to gather testimonies of the repression against the Palestinian people. We found out, through our own experience, that to smell a piece of onion diminishes the effects of tear gas. Rachel Corrie, a young United States hero, was asassinated in 2003 by a bulldozer when she was trying to stop the demolition of Palestinian homes by the state of Israel.

"DIALOGUE WITH ALAIDE FOPPA"
Alaíde Foppa, poet, journalist, art critic, feminist, mother and Guatemalan resistance fighter was kidnapped by authorities in Guatemala at sixty-six, on December 19, 1980. She died in a torture session.

"LA VOZ DE LOS INOCENTES"
Letra de Bernice y Alicia, música de Bernice Johnson Reagon, grabada en el CD *The Women Gather* de Sweet Honey in the Rock (EarthBest, 2003).

"S.O.S"
Con un guiño a Claribel Alegría por su poemario *Umbrales* y otro a María Negroni, por *La jaula bajo el trapo*.

"THE VOICE OF THE INNOCENT"
Lyrics by Bernice and Alicia, music by Bernice Johnson Reagon, recorded by Sweet Honey in the Rock in the CD *The Women Gather* (EarthBest, 2003)

"S.O.S"
Tipping my hat at Claribel Alegría for her *Thresholds* and at María Negroni for her *Cage Under Cover*.

About the Author

Alicia Partnoy is a survivor from the secret detention camps where about 30,000 Argentineans disappeared. She is the author of *The Little School. Tales of Disappearance and Survival*, *Revenge of the Apple-Venganza de la manzana*, and the editor of *You Can't Drown the Fire: Latin American Women Writing in Exile*. She is the Chair of the Modern Languages and Literatures Department at Loyola Marymount University and co-editor of *Chicana/Latina Studies: the journal of Mujeres Activas en Letras y Cambio Social*. She has just launched Proyecto VOS—Voices of Survivors, an organization that brings survivors of human rights abuses to lecture at colleges in the U.S.

About the Translator

Gail Wronsky is the author of three books of poetry, *Poems for Infidels*, *Again the Gemini are in the Orchard* and *Dying for Beauty*, a finalist for the Western States Federation of Arts Poetry Prize. She is also the author of a novel, *The Love-talkers*. Her work appears in a number of anthologies including *Poets Against the War* and *A Chorus for Peace*. She is Director of Creative Writing and Syntext at Loyola Marymount University in Los Angeles.

About the Illustrator

Raquel Partnoy is a painter and art teacher. Born in Argentina, since 1994 she has been living in Washington, DC. Her unique style has matured through more than 50 solo exhibitions and 80 group shows in Argentina and the United States. She has participated in several competitions and received important awards. She has been recognized by Buenos Aires and Washington, DC art critics and her work is found in museums and public and private collections throughout Argentina and the United States. Partnoy received a grant from the Washington, DC Commission on the Arts and Humanities. Her solo exhibitions in Washington, DC include: Parish Gallery; B'nai B'rith Klutznick National Jewish Museum; Embassy of Argentina; Washington, DC Jewish Community Center; The Women's Expo, and Studio Gallery.

CPSIA information can be obtained
at www.ICGtesting.com
Printed in the USA
JSHW040038151222
34894JS00001B/4